SOUL LIFTS

Lin Morel, MA, DSS

Soul Lifts

Lin Morel

Inspired Visionz Publishing

Cover Art ©2014 by Taria Reed Designs

Photo by Lin Morel

Printed in the United States of America

ISBN: 978-1-879672-54-3

www.linmorel.com

Lin Morel

PROLOGUE

In the beginning...

My red Chevy van and I almost ran him over. We didn't know it then, but we were on a crash course with destiny that collided on our way to a story telling workshop. He'd reached the front door of the hotel when he realized he'd left his wallet in the taxi. Cane in hand, eyes focused on the departing cab, he stepped off the curb and into my life. We met upstairs a few moments later when the presenter asked us to introduce ourselves to a person seated nearby. He turned around. I reached out and shook his hand, saying, "Hi, I'm Lin Morel, the lady that almost ran you over."

It's a heck of a way to meet a husband, but it worked for me. And so the incident that could have taken his life gave him a wife. It also blessed me with my third husband and the opportunity to partner with a great man.

This is a love story, and James Stephen Putney is a significant chapter in my life. Our eight years overflowed with loving, miracles, challenges and growth. There was also pain and pleasure, all part of my soul's curriculum. The desired outcome: learning to love myself as if I mattered. Learning to love myself, no matter what. That was and is James' gift to me. He loved me until I could learn to love myself.

Right now, I am missing my friend, my confidant and number one fan. He's no longer in this world, and even now I sometimes feel his silent encouragement to share my life with you. What's present are grief and joy, the paradox of loving and

7

losing and finding more of myself in the midst of it all.

Emotions are boiling like a kettle, bubbling to the surface as I begin the task of putting into words things that are so far beyond words. This is a welcome change to the logic that has protected me for so long from the hurts that I've buried deep within. There is a saying that a sorrow shared is a sorrow halved. I would also say that joy shared is joy doubled.

To live in the past is a cop out. Nostalgia can be addicting. It seduces and tempts us to live in the "good old days." It's tough loving and accepting life on life's terms. It is tougher not to love what's present here and now. That's a fool's job, one that keeps the wheels of hopelessness turning.

Today it feels as though this body belongs to someone else as I allow tears to flow freely, tears that have been suppressed for decades. Tears that speak of liberation from my past as I sacrifice them on the altar of joy. Perhaps my story will liberate you as well and together we can double our joy.

INTRODUCTION
Messages from the Soul

The body stores what isn't released. Understanding this simple truth is a key to freedom. The body is not to be feared. Its energy gives us the ability to live, love, laugh and lead lives of purpose. It graciously stores all our unfinished business until we are strong enough to pay attention to the messages our body sends. An illness or physical challenge is more than a random group of symptoms. They are messages of unresolved issues delivered via our body, meant to awaken us to the habits, beliefs and thoughts which no longer serve us. This is not to say that our challenges will disappear. Rather, we will see them as vehicles for awakening and stepping stones to wisdom.

My challenge, and yours, is to unlock the hidden mysteries that lie beneath the surface of our conscious mind. As we learn to accept, appreciate, honor and cherish ourselves on our life's journey, we begin to allow the truest, most noble and loving "us" to become unfettered. I call that part of us the soul. Others call it spirit. You might call it loving. To me they embrace the three in one.

That is the purpose of sharing my life with you and my journey toward greater loving. Perhaps you will find some similarities. In any event, I offer this book as a gift for your consideration. Take what fits and leave the rest.

SOONER OR LATER

We are called to leave the shore of egoic safety and embark on a journey that takes us where we've never been before. It's a place where we question:

"Who am I?"

"Why am I here?"

Or, deep down:

"How can I make a difference?"

"Do I matter?"

PITFALLS ON THE JOURNEY TOWARDS LIBERATION

We are here to love. The route is fraught with lions, tigers and bears. The lions of the mind roar, "You'll never make it, you're not good enough. Who do you think you are?" The emotional tigers will hunt you down every time you take a risk, always waiting to jump out in the form of those mirroring your hidden hurts and fears. And the bears will as soon eat you as let you pass through the forbidden gates to inner awareness.

When you commit to moving forward, bears awaken from their hibernation to remind you of a million reasons why "you can't." They will distract you with bright shiny objects, or forbidding obstacles like health or financial issues that demand your attention.

The journey toward soul awareness is not for the faint of heart. Lions, tigers and bears, our ego's playmates, can all be used as steppingstones to soul. They are not to be feared — they are to be greeted as strengtheners. It takes great courage to go where our ego cannot go.

Welcome to life as a quest.

Welcome to the world of the ego, our supreme gatekeeper, the one with many faces who knows our secrets and expertly chains us to lives of fear and mediocrity. Ego or soul? That's the mystery, the paradox and the joy of discovering which master you will serve.

This then, is a soul's journey of awakening. Your journey and mine. Let's take it together.

11

Soul Lifts

Approve of yourself. It's the only approval that matters.

SOUL LIFT #1 The Inner Critic

An interesting thing happens when you commit to taking action. Have you ever been stopped in your tracks before you ever got started? Do you know someone who has joined the gym and before the week is out has given up? Ever found the only thing between you and your freshly set goal is that darn cookie, the drink or the desire to please a family member, friend or boss? I have, and I expect you've also had similar experiences.

The intent to begin something new summons the keeper of the first gate. Our ego's gatekeeper appears in the most ordinary of disguises: other things come up, a friend calls, you don't feel like it, you need more education, someone laughs at your intention, etc.

Pretty soon the commitment fades into someday, maybe. That someday may last an entire lifetime. Countless people are left with huge regrets at the end of life. "I wish I'd..." is something I've heard a lot through the years.

Even more challenging is what often happens when we actually take the action toward our goals. Every old story, genetic preconditioning and experience will surface, sometimes all at once! Here's an example that may seem far out or even ridiculous. It happened this morning, the morning after I began writing. It highlights the amazing inter-connectedness of body, mind and spirit.

Hello inner critic!

I finished the first bit of writing and decided to go bed early.

13

About two hours later I woke from a sound sleep with a pounding heart and a racing mind. I watched myself replaying my earlier self-talk as I'd finished the first page. "Well, the first paragraph is okay, but you know you are too wordy. You're too much in your head. Get connected." I got connected, and in came the voice, "You're too emotional." This great inner critic will never give you the approval you seek.

Give your self a break and celebrate when the inner critic stands up and starts shouting. Chances are you're heading in the right direction. It's all part of the process of change and growth. With that reminder, it's move on to another soul lift.

14

SOUL LIFT #3 Life as a Triangle

Here we go! Time to simplify the whole body-mind-emotions-spirit thing.

Imagine a triangle. On one side you write the word action (physical). On another side, feelings (emotions), and on the third side of the triangle, write thoughts (mental). Now imagine the entire triangle filled with spirit. There you have it. The spirit that breathes you connects the fabric of your life.

Your spirit/soul doesn't care what you weigh, or whether you have furrowed brows or glasses. It doesn't care if you act like a drama queen or what your DNA looks like. It doesn't matter if you are smart or not. Spirit just is, permeating everything. What we choose to do with our body, mind and emotions won't change the fact that spirit is always present, even if in the background, ignored and dismissed.

In the best selling book *You Can't Afford the Luxury of a Negative Thought,* author John-Roger says that to be effective we need to line up our thoughts, feelings and actions. They are all inter-connected. If you find yourself spinning your wheels on the way to your goal, chances are you need a physical, mental and emotional alignment.

To keep your ego safe, fear will tell you all sorts of lies about why you can't do something. It's ironic that when you release those fears (often non-productive thoughts, feelings or habitual habits) you find yourself building more self worth and inner strength. It won't matter if you stumble and fall because you are keeping your eyes on your goal.

19

Soul Lifts

Here's a quick story about how I first experienced a life changing alignment. I was 15 years old and my little sister wanted to study judo. I didn't. My parents prevailed and I became her reluctant chaperone. To my surprise, I discovered I loved the sport. I began to see myself in a new, more confident and joyful light. I looked forward to class, the laughter and the learning. My emotions were definitely engaged.

When my sister lost interest, I found myself responsible for getting to class. I used my mental facilities and found rides to the school. I ironed shirts and worked part-time to pay for classes. I was serious about becoming a black belt, even when there were so few women role models. I was willing to pay the price for a heart felt dream that made no sense to those around me. Here I am decades later, still practicing and honing my craft as a martial artist. That initial decision has influenced every area of my life.

Just imagine what you could do if you lined yourself up! Follow your heart and the doors will open. Here's a disclaimer: it may not happen in the way you expect, or in your timing. Trust it's all perfect, and all in your soul's divine hand.

"That which is hidden deep inside of us will manifest itself as fate." Carl Jung

The first five years of a child's life are formative. Our parents' relationship, both spoken and unspoken, creates an energetic container during our early years. If your parents argued frequently or lived in separate bedrooms this became your norm. If one parent was absent, that also is registered as normal. Every nuance of your parents' relationship is filed away for future reference. When we enter into our adult relationships, this original blueprint kicks in.

If you are drawn to one parent more than the other, that parent becomes your role model. You then will unconsciously attract the opposite parent in your own relationships. In any case, you are bound by what you observed and internalized. Add to that the impact of your grandparents' relationships on your parents and you see that there is much more to relationship than meets the eye.

Be gentle, kind and compassionate. With investigation and curiosity you can discover who you are beyond your parental conditioning and break free of the bondage of your past.

SOUL LIFT #4 Time for an Alignment

Let's look at a life challenge from a slightly different perspective and see if we can discover something more about the nature of relationships.

In this analogy, we have a three-sided stool. If you are missing one of the stool's legs it becomes unstable. Said another way, if you fail to align your thoughts, feelings and emotions, you're missing support and may end up on your tush. Which can result in harm (physical), judgment (mental), or embarrassment (emotional).

To support you in your discovery process, I have included a fictional story about a relationship gone bad.

You're in your third relationship in as many years. The relationship breaks up just as things get really good.

Since you are the common denominator in this situation, it is easy to assume that you have something to do with this repeat scenario. You do to a certain extent. Yet, actually, it's not really about you! We human beings learn about relationships from our parents, who in turned learned about them from their parents. Knowing this creates a blame free zone, where we untangle who we are from what we have learned as children. This can be fun, especially when you get the hang of it.

The following example tracks the physical, emotional and mental aspects that appear when we look deeper into the relationship.

Physically: You were really attracted strongly to something about the person. Even though you loved talking on the phone, the great romance and all that jazz, you frequently felt drained when you were together. You also noticed sometimes you were ignored or even on the receiving end of inappropriate comments (at your expense) when you were together in public.

Emotionally: You were SO connected some of the time. You had long talks, shared deeply and saw visions of happily ever after. On the other hand, you noticed that your partner was self-centered. Sometimes they had huge mood swings and got distant. You never knew when the moods would strike. They proposed. Then they told you that you were making a mistake marrying them. You find yourself tending to their every need at your own emotional expense. You are constantly off balance.

Mentally: Impressed with their intelligence, degrees, job or pedigree you ignored all the warning signals from your friends, family and intuition. Your mind said "yes" when your heart shouted "no."

Observation without judgment is powerful. Awareness and acceptance of what we observe is a pathway to transformation.

"You know that our breathing is the inhaling and exhaling of air. The organ that serves for this is the lungs that lie round the heart, so that the air passing through them thereby envelops the heart. Thus breathing is a natural way to the heart. And so, having collected your mind within you, lead it to the channel of breathing through which air reaches the heart, and together with this inhaled air, force your mind to descend into the heart and to remain there."
Nicephorus the Solitary, 13th century monk

The key to living is to keep taking those breaths with as much awareness as possible. When all else fails in life, breathe in and out. If you do that consciously you will find the emotions settle down, the mind slows down and the body relaxes. Nicephorus the Solitary was onto something powerful and gives us a amazing insight into our interior world.

Inspiration can be found in the space between those breaths. It will also refresh you. Ready? Let's take a breath and get started.

SOUL LIFT #5 Simple Stress Relief

Yep, if you're breathing, you're still with us! We can get by for a time without food or water. We don't survive for long without air. A good deep breath can go a long way toward relieving stress. It also oxygenates your body and can be practiced as an inexpensive therapy.

There are many kinds of intentional breathing. Here are several that work for me:

Begin with a sigh or just a plain old exhale. Now allow yourself to receive the next breath without effort. When you have received the breath fully, allow it to release in its own timing. Then allow the next breath to be received into your lungs. This begins a cycle of allowing the breath to naturally flow in and out. Notice the times you hold your breath. This will signal stress or fear and indicate your body's defensive attempt to withhold emotion or self-awareness.

The second technique is a relaxing breath. You can practice it anytime or anyplace when you are feeling out of sorts. Even a few breaths will shift your state into greater peace and calmness. I began using this breathing technique about 27 years ago during my walks after my husband died. Here we go. Breathe in and silently say, "Be Still." In the space between the in and out breath, silently say, "Trust." When you exhale, silently say, "I Am." Repeat until you notice you are feeling better.

Another variation that's fun to use is consciously breathing in through your nose. As you do so, imagine that the air is sliding down the back of your throat, clear down to your pelvis

25

(sometimes I take it right down through my feet and into the Earth). Listen to the sound of your breath sliding down the back of your throat. It will be reminiscent of someone sleeping or deeply relaxed. As you do so, say to yourself, "Be still."

Pause for a moment before you release the breath. Say "trust" inwardly.

As you exhale, allow the air to slide back up your throat and out your nose (If I breathe out the bottom of my feet, I exhale through the top of my head). Silently say, "I am." Both the sound of your breath, and the command, "I am" may create a space for suppressed emotions or fears to reveal themselves.

Once again, pause for a moment before you inhale your next breath. Sometimes I use the word "love."

Practice this gently and kindly with a child's curiosity. Make it okay for your body to release when and as it sees fit. You are also practicing a wonderful affirmation: "Be still, trust, I am. Love." You can also change the word to "peace, heart, acceptance, strong, etc." Experiment and find what works best for you.

Another way to remember the difference between soul and ego is that the ego's job is the process of edging God out. If you don't like the word God, call it edging good out.

Either way, when the ego is in charge, life is a downward spiral. The challenge is not to get rid of our ego. Our job is to love our ego and make it our servant.

The ego will never have an awareness of soul. Soul is eternal. Ego is not.

SOUL LIFT #6 Your Soul's Hidden Agenda

As I began this Soul Lift, I was reluctant to share my personal viewpoint with you. That being said, I got over it, and here it is for you to try on. See if it fits. My perspective allows me to work with myself and others who are dealing with very challenging circumstances. It gives me a different lens with which to view good and bad, right and wrong.

I perceive that every soul has a different curriculum. That curriculum may be hidden from us until we recognize there is more to life than our senses, our culture, our religion or even our experiences and beliefs tell us. My spiritual understanding is this: Nothing we do, nor anything that happens to us matters to our soul. Our soul is here for the experience. It remains neutral no matter what the ride looks like and is loving, no matter what happens.

That brings another question to mind: "If soul/spirit/loving is a foundation for life, why do we have so many challenges?"

The soul is eternal and endless. Since your soul is loving, it loves it all, regardless of the outcomes. Notice I said soul, not ego. It says in the Bible that "God is love." If that is true, and it is for me, then God loves everything equally. Our job is to put the loving where we can't find it. I know it is possible, because I have had plenty of opportunities to look for loving where there seemed to be none. That doesn't make me a Pollyanna; it makes me a realist. The reality is that we are loving, living in human form. When we withhold our loving from anyone, we withhold it from ourselves. That doesn't mean we turn criminals free, nor does it mean we trust strangers, nor give up personal

28

SOUL LIFT #8 Look for the Good

There are many definitions of the word "good," such as the distinction between positive and negative entities; something conforming to the moral order of the universe; praiseworthy character; morally excellent; virtuous; proper; well behaved, to name a few.

Whatever your meaning or context, choosing to put "good" in your life is a key to resiliency. Looking for the good in every situation is a practice, like playing the piano, working on your golf game, or spending time in meditation. It gets easier with repetition.

Sometimes the only thing we can control is our choice to choose how we will respond to what we are experiencing, hearing, seeing, or feeling. We all have days when our practice is off. We can either judge ourselves or let the practice be enough as it is. Up until now, I've never met anyone who consciously says, "Today I'll be a little worse than I was yesterday."

So why not hold a focus of goodness in your everyday coming and going? An entire new world will open up when you choose to look at the mirror of life with curiosity instead of judgment.

Warning! Practice this and you run the risk of feeling better, seeing more clearly, and listening with greater neutrality. And if all else fails, have a piece of chocolate.

Soul Lifts

What are you grateful for?

Make a list, and keep on adding. It's a gift to yourself that will multiply beyond your wildest dreams.

Building a gratitude habit can help prepare you to survive life's storms. If you can't find something to be grateful for right now, make it up! Trust me, gratitude begets gratitude.

Make gratitude your traveling companion. She'll lift your energy in the darkest of times.

To be grateful is not the same as being in denial. Gratitude is what is present, always present, in our times of need. We have only to look for it. That focus shifts our energy into the upward spiral of hope and courage.

34

Lin Morel

SOUL LIFT #9 A Friend Named Gratitude

It was March 10th. The evening before I'd delivered a workshop
to about 60 folks in North Carolina. I woke up early the next
morning and called my second husband, David. Joking around I
said, "I love you madly and miss you badly," to which he replied,
"Get your butt home." So, I got my butt in gear, got in the car
and began an 11-hour journey to a changed life.

I called Dave and left a message giving him a progress report
about half way home. No answer. "Odd," I thought and let the
thought go. Then I had an unmistakable urge to take off my
wedding band. I put it in my dashboard tray. Weird. I hardly
ever took off my ring.

I arrived home at 11:00 p.m. to a pitch black house. David's
jeep was gone. The half done taxes greeted me on the kitchen
table. No sign of my husband. I put my wedding band on the
top of the piano and asked inwardly, "Where's David?" "He's
dead," was the roar that came from my inner silence.

My initial and automatic thought as I dropped into the nearby
chair was, "Thank you for even this." Then a most bizarre
second thought popped in my head. "This is something for your
toolbox. It will someday help others."

My life had changed in an instant. I called the police. They
sent officers to tell me what I had already known. What I hadn't
known is that his ultralight plane malfunctioned. He died doing
what he loved. The days to follow were a blur. I was too numb
to feel much of anything.

It took gratitude to get me through. That and buckets of tears. I pretended I was strong and told friends not to come to the funeral. They ignored me and drove hundreds of miles to comfort me in my time of need. They came and they loved me. They celebrated David's life.

One young man heard of David's death from his counselor, who had brought him for a two day stay at our retreat center. He insisted she bring him to the funeral. They arrived ahead of time and stayed on the property. Walking into the kitchen he filled a bucket with hot water and soap. To my amazement, he got down on his hands and knees and began cleaning my kitchen floor.

I said, "You don't have to do that."

He looked up at me, tears streaming down his face, and replied, "This is how I can tell your husband how much I love him."

We wept together for David's passing.

The loss of my best friend and confidant awakened other deeper losses. The tears were a portent for even more difficult challenges in the coming months.

One day at a time, one moment at a time, I looked for the simple things. I had a roof over my head. Friends came and called. They listened to the same stories over and over. Bless them all.

The gift of grief continued sweeping me clean. My husband's

36

Lin Morel

Guilt prevents us from connecting with our innate goodness.

SOUL LIFT #11 Getting Off the Guilt Train

Find your unconscious beliefs and you begin to loosen the bondage of guilt. Better yet, you might even be moved to forgive yourself and uncover the most precious gift of all: you.

Guilt is defined as "the fact of having committed a specified or implied offense or crime."

There's an irony behind guilt. If you were a sociopath, someone manifesting a personality disorder with extreme antisocial attitudes, behavior and lack of conscience, you probably wouldn't be reading this book, nor would you have a shred of guilt for your actions.

More likely, you are one of the millions of well-meaning individuals who tend to declare themselves "guilty as charged." You might automatically accept other people's projections of their own issues when they pass judgment on your behavior, looks or past.

We often forget that when someone points a finger at us, they are really pointing three back at themselves. It's all about the mirror. What we see in another is always a reflection of some part of ourselves.

With observation, you can begin to get off the guilt train. It might be one trip you'd like to by-pass. To do that you will have to walk through the land of hibernating bears.

42

Remember them? They awaken when you get too close to looking at the root of your behaviors/beliefs/stories and begin moving into the land of authentic observation.

An apology is not an excuse to turn around and break your agreements, the law or repeat the behavior. John-Roger says, "Performance is the best apology."

SOUL LIFT #13 Guilt and the Land of Hidden Beliefs

Here's where we enter the realm of lions, tigers and bears big time. The following is a case study of bears pushing away blessings, courtesy of my aunt Ethel. I'm sure from her heavenly viewpoint she's going, "I get it! So much of my life was about unconscious beliefs and my inability to receive life's goodness."

I like to imagine her giving me a high five. Even if she isn't, I can always high five myself! And so can you. Every step toward greater awareness deserves your own high five. So take a break right now, breathe, and congratulate yourself for your courage. Remember, this is a process of awakening to your soul as love.

The following is a short story about beliefs and prayers.

My aunt and uncle loved going to Las Vegas for their vacation. Almost every year without exception, she would win enough at the slot machines to pay for their trip. They'd return home and help out my mother or anyone else in financial need.

I spent many weekends at their house. Generally I was awakened in the wee hours of the morning to hear her lament from the other bedroom, "I don't know, Unc. There will probably be a lot of taxes on this money. Maybe I shouldn't pray so hard to win.

My aunt punished herself for winning with a litany of negative self talk. Was her glass half full or half empty? She couldn't accept her good fortune as a gift. To add insult to injury, I got

47

the secondhand negativity! Oh well, that's the nature of family. They pass their lessons onto us.

Aunt Ethel was being run over by her unconscious belief system: It's not okay to receive good stuff unless it is for others. It's not okay to pray for your own betterment. If something good happens, the IRS shoe will drop. She couldn't choose to win and by unconscious default lost any goodness inherent in going to have fun with Unc.

She never got to play the game of life without attachment to a negative outcome. In the end, praying was on the agenda, playing was not. Her mega beliefs suggested that good comes with a price tag. No matter what she did, Aunt Ethel couldn't win. When life unfolds that way, you're "Darned if you do and darned if you don't."

Let's listen to our heroine as she handles this going no where fast scenario! She won't mind if we listen in to her process of awakening to her soul's wisdom.

Walking into her dark apartment after work, she realizes it's time for a chill pill. She loves her mom and her friends; it's just they get on her nerves.

"It's time for some self care. I've got to step off the marry-go-round. Let yourself off the hook, Vanessa. You're a beautiful woman. You've grown a lot. You deserve better. When the time is right you'll find the right guy."

"You really wouldn't want to marry a guy who didn't have the courtesy to answer your phone calls or texts. What's wrong with you anyway?"

She doesn't like where her mood is going. It's time for a bath. A candle, some bubbles and a few wonderful oils will work wonders. The sound of the faucet reminds her of the creek where she lived as a child. In a moment of relaxed inspiration she notices that this guy is just like her mom. Yeeks!

Dad always pursued mom. She ignored him. She was too busy with the kids. Even as a child, it was clear to Vanessa that daddy wasn't good enough for mommy. Her mom always said her husband had too many issues. She sadly recalls that there was a lot of finger pointing between her parents. Stony silences were punctuated by shouting matches that came like thunderstorms. Vanessa couldn't remember a single heart to heart communication, or open displays of affection.

55

In spite of all that went on between her parents, Vanessa remembers her daddy with fondness. They walked together in the fields on the days he was around. She wanted to be like him when she grew up.

Oh! In a flash Vanessa becomes aware of something that rocks her world. Not only is her personality like her father, her almost "ex" boyfriend is just like her mother! She's chasing her boyfriend like Dad chased her mom! In a moment of stunning clarity, she just uncovered why this guy seems so perfect. Their relationship was mirroring her mom and dad's relationship with each other.

That moment of self care was solid gold. Vanessa discovered what her unconscious considers to be a perfect fit. For her parents maybe. But not for her. Up until this moment in the tub, she was committed to replicating her parents' relationship with each other.

What you've heard, seen and felt is what you, the little child, was recording in the formative years. Children do as their parents do. Become conscious and awake to your patterns. Look at the parent you felt most comfortable emulating. Recall their conversations and interactions with their spouse. Chances are you attracted the same kind of partner as your role model parent or caregiver. How did your parents treat each other?

Sometimes all you need is a hot bath to let go. All great things happen when you remember the tub and bowl club. And a candle and a few bubbles don't hurt either.

In times of relaxation you make space for your brilliance to surface.

57

Soul Lifts

Have you built a cage around your heart to keep it safe? Is it working? The cage is held in place by habitual feelings and thoughts. Focus on fear and the cage gets stronger. Find the courage to love, and even the strongest bars will fall away.

perspective about turning life's storms into rainbows. Take care of yourself, trust the process, look for the blessing, and you're sure to find a bit of wisdom in the pot of gold at the end of the rainbow.

"A miracle isn't when you get your way but when you get out of your way. Let things unfold how they are meant to, not how we WANT them to." Gabrielle Bernstein

SOUL LIFT #19 No Such Thing as a Small Miracle

When I first read The Course in Miracles in 1985, I found it confounded my thinking. In retrospect, it was a profound opening into greater awareness of a spiritual reality. At that point in my life, logic was both a protector and jailer. I'd never heard nor considered that my mind got in the way of loving, nor that loving was our natural state. It seems odd now, all these years later, to think that something so obvious about loving was such a revelation. The course also taught that miracles are normal and natural, they are an expression of loving, and that prayer is a vehicle.

Miracles are generally thought to occur when they can't be explained by natural causes. Isn't it funny to think that space travel, once the province of fantasy, is an everyday occurrence? Science and miracles do sometimes go together!

I've seen miracles occur when we open to the healing consciousness of our divinity. Miracles are as different as people and our belief systems. One size does not fit all. What does fit is that every miracle seems to bring forward a sense of awe and even reverence for what is possible.

So look. Listen. Feel. Open your eyes, listen with the ears of your heart, and let miracles find you. Your life will never be the same. Consider keeping a miracle journal. If you don't like the word miracle, then consider magic moments. As with anything else, the more you open to experience the wonder of a miracle-filled life, the more you just might discover that everything is a miracle.

64

Lin Morel

Give yourself permission to live from a place of awe. You may find yourself living your life as if it is a miracle. Trust me, it is!

Soul Lifts

Take a break if you're feeling frazzled, tired or out of sorts. Even a few moments can recharge your battery. Your body is a miracle. It knows exactly what it needs. There is nothing noble about neglecting yourself. Ignore your inner wisdom long enough and you may find yourself a burden for those you love.

66

SOUL LIFT #23 Is It Yours?

If you are feeling out of sorts take a moment and ask, "Is this mine?" If it is, then look at what might have opened you to take on the negativity. You can ask things like, "What was the trigger? Is this from or through someone I've met? Is a judgment present?"

If you are pointing the finger of blame or shame, what is the person or issue mirroring back to you? When you take personal responsibility for what you are experiencing, it becomes easier to release the energy that is present and discover where and how the negativity "got in."

For example, one time I found myself judging a guy showing off in the inner courtyard of our local YMCA. I was watching him through the windows as I worked out in the gym. It was a baby judgment and I forgot about it as soon as the thought crossed my mind. About a half hour later I decided to go in the courtyard and stretch and do some tai chi.

The next day I woke up with a backache. It wasn't until I asked where the opening to negativity occurred that I flashed back on the yogi in the courtyard. My own judgment was stuck in my back. Ironically, as soon as I forgave myself for judging him as a show-off, the pain disappeared as quickly as it came.

Conversely, if the issue is "not yours" then ask yourself who you might have been with and what caused you to "take on" their issue. For example, have you ever spent time with a really negative friend and found yourself negative after they left? Here, too, there is an opening to negativity that took you out of

75

your center.

In either case, we have created, promoted or allowed ourselves to be impacted by energy — either our own misdirected energy, or an unintended taking on of someone else's issue.

Get outside whenever you are feeling down. Do what martial artists do and imagine yourself as a tree growing roots into the earth. Draw in the energy and let your body recharge.

Better yet, get barefoot and feel the Earth under your feet!

SOUL LIFT #24 Listen to Your Mother

Native peoples refer to the Earth as "our mother." I've found the earth is an enormous battery that recharges body, mind and emotions. I get out of town into nature as often as I can. A walk in the mountains energizes me. It clears my head and heals what ails me. Time slows down as I calibrate to the Earth's rhythms. Stress dissolves.

Many of us have lost our connection with the Earth, the feel of ground under our bare feet, the coolness from the shade of trees or the magic of our bodies in water. Many children have never seen food being grown. Countless others never play outside after school. There's a huge disconnect from the Earth that feeds and sustains us.

We take the energy of the Earth and our environment for granted. In 2014 I read an issue of AARP's magazine that suggested indoor plants reduce stress by as much as 12 percent — and improve air quality in the office! Flowers lift spirits, as do fragrances. So even if you can't get outside often, find a way to stay connected to your mother.

I keep pictures of nature in my office. I look at the scenes between clients, close my eyes, and imagine myself walking right into the picture. My mood lifts and it's a quick way to "energy up."

What do martial artists, indigenous healers and animals have in common? They connect with the Earth and use her energy. Try it, it's one lift that won't let you down.

Lin Morel

What can't be released is stored.

I know first hand that it does. There was a 13-month period in my life where major events occurred at roughly four-week intervals. I lost my home, my mother, my husband, my livelihood, my health and my daughter. My life resembled a battlefield hospital where there was only enough energy to deal with the most pressing needs. Everything else was relegated to the background.

I was unable to slow down enough to acknowledge the losses as they occurred. The consequence of stuffing unresolved feelings gave rise to a host of health challenges. Add to that unresolved post-traumatic stress and the stage was set for a downward spiral of energy and vitality.

What I learned from that is that if something doesn't kill me, it will make me stronger. I chose to get up one more time than I fell. I still do. I've learned to look at my cup as both half full and empty. Behind every challenge there is a blessing. You can do this too. It's all a matter of energy restoration and honoring everything in your life.

Take a moment just now. Look at your life, and ask yourself, "What area of my life has the least energy?" What would life look like if I took better care of myself physically, emotionally, mentally and spiritually? Pick one area and get going. Do small things over time and you will find the energy wellspring deep within you responding to your willingness to heal and grow.

85

"Joy is not dependent on the information available or even the circumstances or environment. Joy is the underlying foundation that the feeling of happiness skates across." Thelene Scarborough, author of Joy Around Every Corner

"Some of you say, 'Joy is greater than sorrow,' and others say, 'Nay, sorrow is the greater.'
"But I say unto you, they are inseparable.
"Together they come, and when one sits alone with you at your board, remember that the other is asleep upon your bed." Khalil Gibran, The Prophet

86

SOUL LIFT #27 Sing a Joyful Noise

Joy is an interesting creature. Some people radiate joy and their smile lights up a room. Others I've met seem allergic to laughter and joy. Spending time with them seems to dampen the happiest mood.

Joy is an indicator of the presence of spirit. Little children laugh, shout and run around in circles until they collapse laughing at their games. Kittens chase their shadows, and humpback whales breach, slap their tails and spin when set free from fishing nets. I believe we are born with an innate sense of joy. At some point our ability to connect with our joyful self may be lost.

Over the years I've worked with countless people whose joy was set aside as a result of childhood learning and experiences. More than one person has said, "It wasn't safe to be joyful." Others would tell me that a family tragedy or challenge overwhelmed any ability to express joy. All that could be seen was the tragedy. The future became one of looking back to what was lost. Joy somehow became taboo and thought to dishonor the dead or those who suffered.

Happiness, unlike joy, comes and goes with material objects and experiences. We get a new car, a raise, a divorce, or married, we're happy. Joy just is. It emerges when we move beyond separation into oneness. It can't be forced.

If joy can't be forced, it can be encouraged. Taking the time to help someone is a sure way to invite joy to visit. A smile at someone, a kind word or act of kindness invites joy to enter.

87

Soul Lifts

Rabindranath Tagore, the first non-European to win a Nobel prize said, "I slept and dreamt that life was joy. I awoke and saw that life was service. I acted and behold, service was joy."

Heartfelt service is a doorway to joy. Forgiveness and gratitude are also doorways to joy. We can choose to sing a joyful song. Here's a simple one to try on for size. No singing ability required: "Happy, happy, joy, joy. Happy, happy, joy, joy." It's that simple. Even a grump might be surprised when joy appears to lift your mood.

88

Lin Morel

"To let go and let God is to relax and be patient." John-Roger

"Tension is who you think you should be. Relaxation is who you are." Chinese Proverb

SOUL LIFT #28 Are you Past Due for Letting Go?

My neighbor told me once, "I'm really good at holding on and working something until my fingernails crack. How come," she went on to say, "I know letting go is the way to let energy flow and yet I'll want to make something [that's] supposed to be crooked straight. What's that about?"

Questions like that birth awareness. Sometimes we come from environments where we have to work hard to get ahead. When I was a young woman I worked at an engineering company. I handled the purchasing department, mostly because my boss liked alcohol. Most afternoons after a vendor lunch he was unable to make decisions. After a little alcohol he would tell me that women were not cut out to be purchasing agents. Nonetheless, I frequently covered for him, hoping he would notice my good work and promote me to buyer.

So, I worked really hard to be the best. I ran the department, covered for him and made sure the reports were done on time. I even trained the young expeditors and worked closely with the engineers and project managers. I got along great with them.

He wouldn't promote me to buyer. I asked him why. His comment was, "You need to crawl before you walk." I tried harder. Nothing worked. I was trying to make something crooked straight.

One day I got sick and tired of being passed over. It had been more than four years as his secretary. I applied for another position across the street. To my surprise, the interviewer was an old college classmate. I got the job and left my completed

90

resignation on my boss's desk. He didn't sign it right away.

Fate intervened, and my boss got called to personnel instead of me. He was asked to retire. Instead of signing off on my resignation, he promoted me to buyer and left his mark on the department. I thought I was making straight what was crooked.

I still hadn't gotten that it doesn't work to fix what's broken in the first place. I just didn't know it yet! Are you holding on when you're past due for letting go?

91

Soul Lifts

Are you holding to something that's crooked? What keeps you there?

"You got to know when to hold 'em, know when to fold 'em, know when to walk away, know when to run." The Gambler by Don Schiltz, songwriter

SOUL LIFT #29 Ignoring the Expiration Date

Here is more about my staying at a job and ignoring the obvious. The job across the street was history. I'd gotten my wish. I was a buyer. Imagine a petite little thing buying pipes, valves and fittings. Not to mention rebar and assisting with instrumentation and the purchase of heat exchangers. I thrived, or so I thought.

Then one day, fate intervened again in the form of a head hunter. He contacted me and asked if I was open to an interview. "Why not?" I thought. "I've been here five years. Maybe it's time to see what else is out there."

Two days before my interview I was at the Akron Ohio National AAU Karate Championships. I placed as the third ranked female fighter in the United States and came home with a heck of a shiner. Not exactly how I'd planned to impress my potential employer.

Guess it did the trick. I got the job. Being hired as a project manager in charge of supplying building materials for Riyadh, Saudi Arabia, seemed like a dream come true. I also found my first job had severely underpaid me. I loved the raise and the title.

The first day I started work my secretary quit. The next day the expeditor left. Things went downhill from there and before long I was chief cook and bottle washer.

The overt hostility at work was palpable. After the first six weeks at the job, I was the second most senior person in the

93

company other than the owners. When I looked in the mirror one morning, I'd aged at least 10 years. I was ignoring the expiration date, so my body gave me the message loud and clear. In a freak accident when I was teaching my karate class, I tore the ligaments in my knee. It was time for me to leave that job, but I didn't know how.

Sometimes we stretch ourselves like Silly Putty trying to fit the situation. Then we get stuck with the silly sublime in the form of a lesson unlearned.

It is really helpful to look at your growth in terms of doing your best. When the light turns on to reveal an unhealthy environment with unhealthy people, you might just want to take your Silly Putty and play elsewhere. Remember, there is no real failure in life, only lessons. What you get, no matter what the outcome, is the opportunity to learn and grow.

94

Lin Morel

If you ignore the obvious signs that something needs to change in your life, you may end up with a heavenly 2 x 4 that will shake things up and get you moving. It may be heavenly but it still hurts.

95

SOUL LIFT #30 Letting Go, Yes, No, Yes, No Way!

I hadn't entertained the idea of quitting my project manager job. I was out of my league and loyal where loyalty was not called for. Employees were shell-shocked by the owners' outbursts. I was only three months on the job. The only person who would talk with me was the purchasing agent. The staff lived in fear of leaving their desks, even for lunch. They arrived early and worked late. Heaven intervened in the form of my knee injury. It was an old-fashioned God-incidence in action that helped me wake up to the level of stress in my life.

I was in a leg cast for my knee injury at the local diner with my first husband, Peter. I looked at the table across from us and there was the second-in-command at my old job. He came over and said, "We miss you, Lin. Won't you come back? They've hired a new head of purchasing. I'll arrange for an interview."

Wow. Nirvana, or so I thought. The very next week I met the new department head. I walked in his office and the first thing he said was, "You'll have to start from the bottom again. You must pay the price for leaving. No vacation, no insurance." He went on to say, "I don't like lesbians." He made that amazing connection because I happened to be wearing a suit. He told me to my face.

That comment was beyond anything I had ever heard. It was a power play made by an egotistical human being who didn't have a clue. I didn't need the job that much.

I stuck my head in my friend's office, saying, "I should sue this company for what just happened." I marched straight down to

96

the personnel office in tears and let them have it.

Ironically, I got the job. I got my three weeks vacation back and immediate restoration of my health care and time off to repair my knee.

I loved my friends and colleagues at that company and it was good to be back. There are always people who demean, criticize and project their own issues. You'll find them everywhere. I do my best to let go of what others say about me and hold on to the fact that what others say about another is a reflection of what they are saying about themselves.

Do you take things personally rather than see it is someone else's stuff? Do you hang on when you should let go? Be willing to let yourself know the truth. That's a great first step. Then do the one thing that will help you take inspired action to change your outcome.

Get curious when circumstances in your work/life seem totally wacky or cultures collide. Explore how you can turn something into a win-win for all parties concerned. Don't take anything personally! Look for common ground and shared values. You may notice that paying attention to, and addressing, the unspoken needs and feelings will turn things around rapidly.

When all else fails, you can resort to a silent prayer, "God bless you. I love you. Peace, be still." Repeat often! The results are powerful and transcend our mind's ability to figure things out. God bless you is a powerful commandment that harnesses spiritual energies. I love you also refers to loving the divinity of that person (not their personality) and peace, be still is a spiritual commandment that helps to bypass the ego's desire for drama and control. These nine words fill the space with loving for every aspect of your circumstances.

SOUL LIFT #31 Bridging Two Worlds

Ah, the joys of being a woman in a man's world circa 1978. I got the buyer's job no one else wanted. I guess they thought I'd quit. Instead, I was determined to succeed and worked twice as hard to make sure I covered my bases. I wanted to make sure the biased department head had nothing to complain about.

I was assigned to work on an Indian project. We corresponded by Telex and all was well. They referred to me as Mr. and I never thought to correct their error. It didn't seem important.

Then they sent a contingent of engineers to visit our office and all H... broke loose.

They didn't know what to do with me. There was no protocol for dealing with a woman buyer. The engineers demanded that a man attend every meeting with me. I felt invisible. It was as though they couldn't hear what I said. Something divine was sparked during this crazy set-up. After two meetings the male buyer just excused himself and left the meeting. Tentatively we continued our conversation. A bridge had been built.

As the shock wore off, the engineers came to value my work. I was no longer "the woman." I was Lin. In fact, they began letting their colleagues know in advance what they would meet on the other end. Working twice as hard had done it's magic. They let go of the fact I was a woman when they found they could count on a job well done. In my own way I had helped to bridge two differing cultures.

99

Soul Lifts

Life is about change. Some things are eternal; other things are not. I believe loving, caring, sharing, health, wealth and happiness are all things we can create through our choices. It is much easier to practice when we live life in alignment with our soul's purpose. These ways of being are internally generated and require a commitment.

There are times to speak, and times to hold our tongue. There will always be those who use their power to put you down and those who are afraid of what they don't understand.

Wisdom comes from learning to listen inwardly and trusting that things will eventually work out for our highest good. Hold the best vision you can imagine, keep your feet on the ground and your head held high. Believe things always work out for the best, act as if they already are, and you'll find transitions a whole lot easier.

SOUL LIFT #32 Sometimes Letting Go Needs a Little Help

I'd been at my company for eight years. I was working with engineers from Uttar Pradesh in Northern India. We were getting along just fine. Life was pretty good in the career department. I didn't know it, but things were about to shift again.

After more than a decade of married life I found out I was expecting a child. I knew it had to be kept secret, since in the early 80's the thing that a male-dominated engineering company dreaded was a pregnant woman! Luckily, it looked like I was gaining weight. No one asked and I kept the news quiet. I'd often heard the rationale that women were a waste of training, since they inevitably resigned their position to start a family. Late in my pregnancy I was asked if I would transfer to Belgium for a year. If I'd been single I would have jumped at the chance. I said no. They still didn't know about my little one.

By this time, the department head had grudgingly come to respect my work. I was in demand as a buyer on the India Project. My Indian friends always wanted me to handle their requisitions. It saved my job several times when there were multiple lay-offs in my department.

This time I wasn't so lucky, or was I? My boss gave me a weird look as he left early that afternoon. Moments afterwards, the second-in-command called me into his office. "Lin, I'm sorry we'll have to let you go." They had me pack up my desk and leave. No time given for goodbyes or closure. It was just time to move on. That was fine by me. I had a month off before my precious little girl was born.

101

Soul Lifts

What I was beginning to see was that there is an order to the universe. Change is constant, and even the most wonderful job has its expiration date. Dancing with change with gratitude in our hearts makes transitions so much easier.

102

There are bullies in life. There are those that see injustice and shrug their shoulders or turn away, not wanting to get involved. Sometimes the only way out is to stand your ground. Choose your battles wisely, cover your butt with documentation and do what you have to do to make it right. What doesn't kill you makes you stronger.

SOUL LIFT #33 Overcoming Prejudice

My second husband, David, used to tell me, "Choose your battles wisely." He was right. Battles take a lot of energy but sometimes you need to call a spade a spade. There are times to speak up when the unspeakable happens.

I have a wonderful friend who is a critical care nurse. Boy, I'd want her on my side if I ever had to navigate the chaos of emergency medicine. What an advocate. On more than one occasion, her intuition saved the day and the lives of those she served.

When she first said, "This one is going to code. Pay attention."

Her co-workers scoffed at her and replied, "Who do you think you are, the angel of death?" No more. They no longer say, "Don't be ridiculous." Instead, they say, "Okay, we will." And they do.

One time her life was going to code in a way that would seriously jeopardize her professional future. It didn't happen in the ER, it happened in graduate school. No one listened when she asked for help in dealing with an unfair professor. She spoke up, she wrote, she pleaded. They dismissed her every time she reached out. The ongoing incidents continued to be swept under the rug.

At one point they recommended she seek council to help shift her behavior, perception and attitude toward the injustice that was being perpetrated. When she persisted, she was told, "Go see the dean." She went to see the dean and he suggested that

104

if she wanted to pass the class it was up to her to find a way to make it work.

She couldn't work something that was stacked against her. She refused to code. Life on the streets of Detroit taught her that she needed to be as fierce an advocate for herself as she was for her patients.

I'm happy as a clam that she's my neighbor. My life is so much richer with her in it! She took on the bully and stood up in the face of institutional prejudice. It didn't matter that there was outright refusal by the countless people she asked to assist her in getting a fair shake. She got set up, set aside and she in turn sat them down.

Sometimes a woman's gotta do what she's gotta do. My friend took her case to the Department of Education. Fifteen months of standing tall and the truth came out. That stand for truth rectified the un-truth of bias and ignorance. And as a really amazing postscript, a peace came over her after she filed her case. She knew deep within it would turn out for the best. It did, and the ripple effect will touch many other lives.

Spend time and write down your heart's desire. If you commit it to paper, it takes on a life of its own! It's especially helpful to write for the highest good of all concerned. There may be a few major details you've forgotten! If your requisition is for a relationship, don't forget to say available. If it's for a job, a new car or something you want, bring it inside of you and live as if you already have whatever you seek. Wanting something may lead to perpetual longing. It puts it outside of you, and therefore separate from you.

If you hold on too tight, you push away the very thing you say you want. If something is yours, it will appear, frequently when you least expect it. Become the one you seek and treat yourself as your own lover. Then, you're more likely to recognize the gift when it is delivered. Add to that a healthy dose of patience and remember that if you are calling for someone to come to you, they are a work in progress as well! Divine timing has a divine sense of humor! Ironically, the same goes for your job, your career and every aspect of your life.

SOUL LIFT #34 In the Beginning was the Word

Words are powerful and create our future. They plant seeds that will manifest in a timing that may not be what we expect, or even prefer! For example, I met my third husband, James, years after I'd written down a description of my ideal next relationship. In the intervening time since David's death, a long-term relationship had faded far from my conscious desire.

My to-do list got a radical revision in January 1999 at the National Speaker's Association Annual Convention in Anaheim, CA. I wandered into a talk about Feng Shui, the art of arranging your environment so that the energy flows gently and smoothly. I wasn't terribly interested. I just wanted a place to sit for a while, so I sat next to the room monitor on a chair in the back of the room.

Suddenly my body, quite independent of my mind, snapped to attention as the speaker said, "Who here wants a red hot relationship?" In a flash, I find my hand in the air. Just as quickly I take it down. Too late, the damage was done. The speaker invites me to the stage. In front of 200 or so fellow speakers, she asks me to describe my red hot guy.

My rapid-fire answer was something like this:
• He loves God first, himself second and me equal to himself.
• He has an active spiritual life.
• He's intelligent, articulate, good looking in my eyes.
• He's romantic, honest, kind.
• He loves kids and animals, even if he doesn't have any.

107

- He is monogamous, sexy as can be and an amazing lover.

- We're compatible physically, emotionally, mentally and spiritually.

- He's healthy and has a great sense of humor.

- He loves nature, music and books, adventures, learning and dancing.

- He's compassionate, considerate and accepts me as I am.

- He loves to touch and be touched.

- He lives life in harmony with service and soul.

- He's done deep inner work and is self aware.

- He's a great all around person, wonderful and trusted friend.

- He's everything my heart desires and more, for the highest good of all concerned.

When I was done rattling off my list she said, "That was amazingly clear. When do you want it by?"

The date July 31st flew into my head. I kept that date to myself and said, "By December 31st of this year."

Well, when you're lined up, the stars are lined up and your future husband is lined up and looking for you things can

108

happen fast.

Ironically, the man of my dreams was already in my life. I just
didn't know if when I got on stage. I'd met him just 24 hours
earlier when he stepped off the curb in front of my van. We
were married on July 24th, six months after we met. Why not
the 31st? His brother couldn't get the day off work to be James'
best man. Turns out my arm in the air knew something I didn't
know. The description I'd written down all those years earlier
had come to fruition at last.

Soul Lifts

If you have had a loss and find it hard to love, consider getting a pet or a plant. When you take care of something, magic happens. If you don't want to have a dog or cat or even a plant, make friends with the ones in your neighborhood. If you have even a little willingness, loving will work her magic.

SOUL LIFT #35 The Cat Who Opened My Heart

Before meeting James, my sweet husband number three (Lord that sounds so abundant), I had a few years with a shut down heart. David's death had brought many gifts. One of them was the gift of courage to look at my life more deeply. Grief had carved out great new spaces inside of me. My heart, however, refused to open to loving another person.

I talked the good talk. I had even dated a guy or two. But deep down I wasn't having any of this open up and lose again stuff. It was a pattern that I was both resisting and denying.

It took a stray cat to open my heart. His name was Nubie. Nubie adopted my friend Paul when he walked into Paul's back porch one day and stayed, in spite of the other cats already in residence. Soon afterwards, Paul's significant other called me out of the blue to say that they were coming over with a surprise. Good thing he didn't say it was a cat. A few hours later they showed up at my door with cat, cage, food and toys. Before I could say no, they dropped him, saying, "Keep him for a night." What a night! He scratched and meowed his way into the wee hours.

The reason I decided to keep him at all was something that preceded his arrival. The night before Nubie made his grand entrance, I'd invited some friends of over for dinner.

Out of the clear blue my friend Anita said, "Do you have a black cat?"

"Heck, no. I don't want any animals. Too much trouble."

111

"Well," she said, "Spirit is showing me a black cat with green eyes. It has a really long tail that wraps around his front paws. He's sitting in your living room looking at us."

"Anita," I said laughing. "No way am I getting a cat."

Never say never! When Nubie arrived the next day, he fit that description to a "T." We became inseparable. My heart softened as I let my regal Burmese rule the roost. My heart was on the mend.

Lin Morel

Life's deepest tragedies leave your earth scorched. New life will occur. It's a part of the normal cycle of birth, growth, death and rebirth. Our job is to look for the new growth and nurture it. Have faith in your future, open up to the possibilities that faith in yourself is a key to new life.

113

SOUL LIFT #36 An Ode to Faith

There once was a little soul named Faith who decided to pick Kenya as her mother. Just after her conception, Faith's mother-to-be began having a rough time in relationship with her husband. Little Faith, conceived in loving, had come on a mission to awaken her mom to the nature of loving from the inside out. Still in the womb, Faith became a guiding light for her mother-to-be as she navigated her pregnancy. No matter how difficult her environment was with her husband, Kenya felt the love of this little soul.

What Kenya didn't know is that Faith was on loan from God. The little one had come to help her mother get strong and learn to love herself. Little Faith also had her own soul's lesson, which was to let go when that job was done.

Faith completed her assignment before she was born into the world. The seeds for her mama's transformation had been planted. It was in Faith's death that her purpose for living was fulfilled. Faith had come to give her life that her mother might find her own soul's purpose and direction.

Kenya's stillborn child left her mother wide open to the miracle of life, death and transformation. Kenya understood she couldn't have her baby back. The thought of losing "her only love" consumed her at first. Eventually that same loving she felt from her daughter's presence, no matter how short lived, helped Kenya through the valley of the shadow to the other side and into the light of a new beginning. Part of that new beginning was to divorce her husband.

114

During the difficult times that followed, Kenya often wrote in her journal. She courageously examined her own lack of self esteem, feelings of unworthiness, separation and isolation.

On one dark night, she called out for help, writing, "Something must give. I deserve and desire better. I am asking you, God, to elevate me and make my goals attainable. I know that no one but you has brought me this far."

Kenya's prayers for self esteem were answered in time and she gave birth to a non-profit called FIG or Faith in Girls. Today, little Faith lives on in every young woman who gets a second chance to grow into the experience of a strong self esteem. Today Kenya has lots of girls, all named Faith. To learn more go to www.Faithingirls.org.

Soul Lifts

Do you love getting up in the morning? Do you embrace life's adventures and look at everything as an "upgrade" or do you dread change? If not, you might be playing it safe. Safety is never safe. It leads to a routine. Routines kill creativity and keep us small. So be bold, be brave and be bodacious. It's your life and your genius that will get you where you want to go. If you couldn't fail, who would you be and what would you do?

SOUL LIFT #37 Genius Leaves Clues

Do you sometimes feel clueless about your next steps in life? Do you face hard decisions without an easy resolution? Ever feel like you don't fit in? Are you a stranger in a strange land? My guess is yes!

You're not alone. We are all strangers in a strange land, and I believe that may occur as a result of growing up in social structures that celebrate conformity. In graduate school I read an interesting study that found approximately 97 percent of four-old children tested at the genius level. I interpreted that knowledge by saying they were, "just being themselves." Those same children were retested again at age seven. The results were astounding. The percentage of genius level had dropped to between three and four percent!

The Latin root of the word genius means, "guardian deity or spirit, which watches over each person from birth," or "innate ability." By the time we're 12, most of us have sacrificed our genius on the altar of peer approval. We do our best to fit in. We begin to worship the god of others' opinions.

If your life isn't working for you, it might be time to step back and ask if you are living from your own inner truth. Do you say "yes" when your heart screams "no?" Do you cover up your feelings, ignore your inner wisdom and sell yourself out for the job, the promotion, the relationship?

Stop pretending you are anything but divine. You are one of a kind. The clue you seek may be deeply buried, denied and covered over by your life's experiences and beliefs. Begin to

117

honor and accept your innate ability and let your soul's genius lead you home. The world is waiting for you.

Are there people that make you nervous? Next time you get a chance, really connect with someone. Listen with respect. Allow yourself to stand in their shoes and see through their eyes. Differences may end up being similarities. Love is love, no matter how you slice it. Ultimately, it is love that binds us together.

SOUL LIFT #38 A Higher Perspective

Sometimes a little perspective goes a long way. Everyone has a viewpoint, whether they share it or not. When we refuse to see the other person's point of view or make snap judgments based on appearance, religion or even their past, we close ourselves off to the magic of diversity. That's a quick recipe for trouble.

Differences and diverse opinions keep us from getting bored. So the next time someone disagrees with you, perk up and get curious. Ask them to tell you more about why they believe what they do. Curiosity doesn't have to kill the cat; it can ignite finding common ground.

Ignorance kills loving. We fear what we don't know. We want to control so we feel safe. Often, we spout others' opinions rather than do the work to have our own. Often, we point our fingers at our friends, or enemies, and make comments about their beliefs or opinions. What I've learned is that when we point the finger at someone else, three are pointing right back at us!

Get out of the safety zone and into the human zone. You might make a few new friends.

That is exactly what happened when I was at an event in support of ending domestic violence. There were a few men in the audience. One of them stood out and looked downright scary. He was a huge guy covered in tattoos, dressed like a biker and someone I would normally give a wide birth. Instead we were paired up. When I looked past my immediate intimidation I found the most gentle, caring and committed young man. He was a child of domestic violence and had come

to help end it. The National Coalition Against Domestic Violence and FBI Crime Statistics share that, "63% of boys, age 11-20, who commit murder, kill the man abusing their mother." That young man escaped that statistic and was truly inspirational in his proactive desire to heal his past and commit to a better future for children.

There is great truth to the saying, "Don't judge a book by its cover." So too, let's not judge another until we get to know them. There is also another truth that says, "We are all one. What you see in another must exist in you, or you would not see it."

121

Soul Lifts

Most of us live in a trance, unaware of why we do what we do, failing to see the obvious. Unleash your hidden programming; your actions speak louder than words. If you want to know what you believe, just watch what you do.

"You see, my dear Watson, but you do not yet observe."
Sherlock Holmes in *Hound of the Baskervilles*

SOUL LIFT #39 Your Perfect Mate

If you want to attract the perfect mate, begin with yourself.

Do you want an honest, open and committed man (or woman)? Be honest, open and committed to yourself. Become what you want to attract.

That is sometimes easier said than done. I've discovered, through the insightful work of Anne Teachworth, that we must repair our parents' relationships if we are to attract our "perfect mate." Like it or not, as children we imitate our parents' relationship. Their relationship becomes the model for our future relationships. Unconsciously, we become like our father and/or mother. Unknowingly, we grow up to live out their lives instead of our own. The way they expressed their relationship becomes exactly the kind of relationship we see and attract. No matter how dysfunctional it may be, it's our normal because it was what we knew.

The way to break this deep-seated learning is to take the time to discover how you were programmed to see relationships. Then recreate your parents' relationship. Yes, you can redo the past!

Win in your own fantasy. Do you want a guy that loves and adores you? If your mama and papa didn't adore and love themselves and one another, you won't change your future unless you change their past.

Look at the relationships you've had. Have you recreated your mother or father's relationship? Look for the patterns…they're

123

golden opportunities to discover how to attract your perfect mate, not your parents. And, ironically, even if you haven't met your birth mother or father, you still mimic their relationship unconsciously.

Check out Anne Teachworth's book, *Why We Pick the Mates We Do*, 1997, Gestalt Institute Press, Metaire/New Orleans, Louisiana, USA, to get her in-depth approach to healing. You may also want to find a therapist versed in Gestalt therapy or someone you trust who can move you into greater conscious awareness of your patterns.

Loving is queen. Asking is king. Sooner or later you will feel safe enough to bring the unconscious to light. Change happens organically when we don't try to push the river.

SOUL LIFT #40 The Truth, the Whole Truth

"No matter how bitter the taste, truth always gives a better meal than dishonesty." My new neighbor, Kenya, read this from her journal as she shared the passing of her daughter, Faith.

The truth will set you free. It's also a bitter pill to swallow. Let's admit it, we lie to ourselves a million times a day. It's a way of life. We promise, "I'll go to the gym tomorrow. I'll stop beating my wife. I won't get angry again with my kids. I'll lose that weight." On and on we go. Mostly we lie to ourselves. Do that often enough, and it gets easier to lie to others. Before you know it, life may become a merry-go-round of deception.

When we place demands on our self to change something that just won't change, I've found that the unconscious doesn't feel safe enough to let the situation release. That in turn tells me that we need to build a bridge between the conscious and unconscious parts of ourselves that are in opposition. Truth connects the two.

To turn our obstacles into steppingstones and allow our best self to emerge, we need to gain access to our unconscious and reprogram it. Trouble is, it is normally out of reach. You can't go at it directly. What you can do is watch what you say and pay attention to what you do. Everything leaves a clue! There are varying shades of truth. What was taken as true when you are young may be very different than the truth you would see as an adult. That bridge helps us to find the deeper truth and release something that once served us. When it no longer does and we look for the deeper truth, we find a path to freedom from the bondage of old decisions that have since been taken as "truth."

Lin Morel

Become kind and compassionate to yourself and others. Give yourself and others a break when they fall short. Habits and the unconscious are stronger than willpower. You can grit your teeth and walk away from the cake for only so long. Sooner or later your unconscious will have its way. That's just the way it is until you become a little more conscious about the reasons you and others behave in ways that aren't productive.

To change your unconscious, become a detective. Get curious and ask yourself, for example, "What is my willingness to change this pattern on a scale of 1 - 10?" If you find yourself at a 0.5, don't panic. It is wonderful that you got an answer.

Ask yourself another simple question, "Am I willing to move that dial by .5%?" That's a really small change. Then you acknowledge that inner part that was willing to shift. Little by little, you encourage that part to become visible. If it won't shift, love it anyway. Keep checking in, stay curious and sooner or later you will find a core issue. Better yet, you will be able to replace it with something that lifts you to a new perspective and outcome.

127

Soul Lifts

If you want a miracle, try a perspective break.

Take time out to slow down and look closely at what's really going on in your life. Ask for the highest good, and that only the highest good, to come into your awareness. Set your inner critic on the sidelines before you begin!

Enlarge the situation in your mind's eye so you can walk right inside it to the center of your area of concern. Slowing down this way will make it easier to see details that might have been missed.

Then imagine yourself rising above the situation to get an aerial view of the same challenge. It's a simple process.

When you take the time to shift your perspective to other viewing points, you open the door for new solutions.

SOUL LIFT #41 Moving Too Fast

When your exterior moves faster than your interior, something gets lost in the shuffle. That's you, your very essence. It's subtle and you need to pay attention to that still small voice within.

We live in a society that rewards doing instead of being. Yet "ing" implies action. We are doing, going, coming, producing, sleeping and loving. Being is a state of the inner Beloved. It's a little like the eye of a storm. Everything rages outside the center. In life's storms, if we go to the center things will get quiet. You get more done. Life gets simpler. Your values and priorities awaken and gain more clarity. You step free of the countless distractions that pull you in different directions.

Here's what a friend shared about the subject of moving too fast: "Don't forget your life when you overreact. Know your worth, embrace your purpose, accept the journey. From one event to another, the time in between seems so silent and yet, a time for focus and cautious walking. You can only do what you can do. You can't make people be something they are not, and you cannot make them react within your expectations. What you can do is see the situation, trust your instincts, and place yourself exactly where you need to be."

I couldn't have said it better myself. Become aware of what drives you. Are you over reacting because you're tired or invested in what other's say or think? Do you need to stay in control?

Perhaps you're a lot like me. I used to "major in the minors,"

129

always taking care of others, never taking the time to feel the intense emotions that were held at bay for fear of being overwhelmed. Thank goodness life slowed me down so I could begin to discover what was really meaningful. My wish is that you slow down so you can be present moment by moment to the wonders of life. The fear of overwhelm is just that — a fear that will distract you from the amazing being you are.

If your parents or grandparents are alive, consider asking them about their childhood, their challenges and triumphs. If they are gone, do something radical. Get really still, put out two empty chairs, and sit in the chair of the person who has passed away. Let them speak through you. Then you will alternate back and forth between your chair and theirs. This is called a gestalt. Your body knows because they still live inside of you.

SOUL LIFT #42 The Gift of Knowledge

I sometimes say, "Thank you for the gift of knowledge." We can learn from history if we pay attention to patterns and trends in our lives. When we open up to something beyond the norm, we may find our ancestors are calling to us. Their DNA runs through our body, shaping how we respond to life. We can't change our DNA. We can change how we express our genes. We can also grow from our ancestors' challenges, their blessings and their wisdom.

I have worked with many people who do not know their fathers or mothers. Their life feels chaotic and they can't find their roots.

You can find them if you get silent. If your ancestors came from Europe or Africa or Asia or the rest of the world, learn about your culture, even if you are American. You will find a certain comfort connecting to your heritage.

Recently I talked with a woman who was raised Catholic. She says she has always identified with the Jewish religion. When we had dinner recently, she shared that she was adopted when she was three months old. Her mom kept her for six weeks. When she released her daughter to an orphanage, she specified that her child be placed in a Catholic home.

My friend spent years searching for her mother. Finally she found her birth mom's family, but it was too late. Her mother had just passed away. The mother's sister hung up on her, saying, "It's too painful to talk about. Just forget it." My friend was devastated. She waited a year, wrote a letter or two, and

132

built up her courage to call again.

This time, a man answered the phone. She begged to know the truth. Here's what she was told. Her mom was a good Catholic girl post WWII in Europe. She had a one-night affair with a young Jewish man. She got pregnant and never told him. She gave her baby away even though she loved her.

Finally my friend had her answer. She'd known she was Jewish from the inside out. The ancestors had brought to light the deeper truth of who and where she came from. Her inner wisdom had guided her to the truth she had suspected all along.

Soul Lifts

It doesn't matter if you are a king or queen, a pauper or a prostitute. When it is your time to leave this life nothing will keep you here. Our final exit is non-negotiable. Death is the great equalizer. Consider breath as another name for God, Higher Power or Source.

Lin Morel

SOUL LIFT #43 The Great Equalizer -- God

I can hear some of you saying, "I don't like the word God." Get over it! Substitute a word of your choice. What I'm talking about is something bigger than you or me. It's the something that breathes you. It is beyond religion, culture, the mind, emotions or the body.

What breathes you? Hold your breath until you pass out. Something breathes you. When you are on your way out of this world, all your desire to keep breathing won't work.

So, you might as well ask for "It" to be your partner. It is anyway. Cooperate with your breath. That makes life easier. It's also one of the greatest gifts you'll ever receive.

135

Is there one particular area where you excel in the complaint department? If you are willing to experience discomfort, this is a rich area of exploration.

What need isn't being fulfilled?

What expectation do you have that may be limiting your ability to find a solution for your complaint?

Take responsibility that in some way or fashion you are creating, promoting or allowing this to continue. What's the payoff?

136

SOUL LIFT #44 I Want to Complain

Give yourself a break. You're human, and everyone has one of those days. Misalignment happens. Sometimes you can't figure out how to get back to basics. Highs and lows, valleys and peaks are all part of our journey.

Let love come to visit. Know that love delivers. It's just not always in your timing or the way you want it.

So love it all -- the good, the bad, the ugly. It's all just the stuff of life. If you can't find any loving in the situation, put it there yourself. As my teacher John-Roger used to say, "Win in your own fantasy."

Love yourself when you complain. Accept your friends when they complain. That doesn't mean you have to hang around them. Take care of yourself first.

It's a little harder to walk away from yourself. That's where compassion comes in. Give your inner complainer a voice and an opportunity to receive a little loving. Lastly, change your complaining ways with the antidote: some gratitude and appreciation for who you are, the way you are. You are enough.

Soul Lifts

There's a time and place for everything. Living in the flow is a sure sign you're on your right path. Trust your process and know that life is filled with cycles and seasons that come and go.

SOUL LIFT #45 Contentment, a Double-edged Sword

Contentment is a wonderful thing. We accept what we have and appreciate life. Things are flowing and there is harmony in and around us. Life may not be what we prefer, yet we accept what comes.

I spent years chasing contentment and running from domestic upheaval. I had fleeting glimpses when I read books and imagined myself the protagonist, the heroine or the one solving mysteries. Chaos disappeared when I stepped into the world that appeared between the pages.

Chaos also disappeared when I started working out, training my body and mind. I felt safe in the dojo (gym), surrounded by a community of people who honored me as I was. Beginner, intermediate, advanced were all acceptable places to find contentment. What I was really finding was that I was more than a mind. I knew that if I honed my physical skills things would improve. There was always a new horizon, a greater level of proficiency, and an opportunity to stretch my limits. I found an outlet for the anger, grief and confusion that held me hostage and spirited away my contentment.

Yet, what I discovered is that within contentment lies the seed for discontent. It's like the yin and yang in the tai chi symbol. Within light is a small aspect of darkness and within darkness is an aspect of light. It is so easy to begin to compare our practice to others, to judge ourselves as not enough. We may also become complacent when we win a tournament, get accolades or trophies.

139

Soul Lifts

Balancing contentment and learning is a part of evolution. There is a time in life where learning and growing is natural. Then we consolidate with times of contentment. To be stagnant leads to decay. Our spirit longs for more. Life is a cycle of growth and rebirth.

Looking to express more in life is what drives inventions, books, poetry and music. We long to express our soul in this adventure called life.

Celebrate your life as if everything is for your good. If you can't find the good, put it there. Emotions, thoughts, pains, shames, joys are all grist for the mill. No one emotion is better or lesser than the other. They're all energy in motion.

SOUL LIFT #46 Good Stuff

Why is it that it's sometimes easier to focus on what's wrong rather than what's right? I sit here on Christmas Eve contemplating the many miracles that appeared this past year. It was a challenging year on many levels. My brother almost died, I lost lots friends to death, and business is interesting, to say the least.

It is a time of reinvention.

Good stuff comes when we accept where we are. No apologies, no excuses. Life unfolds with the breath as our partner. Love it all. That's all you have.

Choice is the thing that separates us from our friends in the animal kingdom. The so-called lesser creatures all sing God's praises. All you have to do is hear a warbler sing in the spring, or listen to a frog ribbit. Cats meow and mice squeak. They sing their song of creation. Even grasshoppers rub their legs together and make their sound.

The good stuff comes when we proclaim life good. Within every moment we have a choice to declare, "It is good. It is God." God and good are only a vowel apart.

So it's all good stuff: crying, laughing, living, dying. It's just a part of being human. Enjoy it all. It's your life.

Loss is a fact of life. It's part of the cycle of creation.

Are you holding on to your past? Sometimes talking about it with someone will help you release unprocessed emotions.

Don't be afraid to let others help. Learn from the experience. Only you can pick yourself up and choose to see everything as an action of goodness.

SOUL LIFT #47 What's Love Got to Do with It?

Tina Turner made those words famous. My take on the song is a little bit different. Love has everything to do with it! You've probably also heard "love makes the world go round" or "love until it hurts," or many other variations, positive or negative.

What if love is the glue that holds creation together? What if love raises the sun, helps a mother get up in the middle of the night to feed her baby or walk the floors when her spouse is ill? What if love has your mate go to work every day to help provide for the family? What if love has total strangers rush into a burning building to save a child?

Love is the foundation of our world.

"What?" you say. "What about all of the killing, the wars, famines and tragedies that strike innocent people?"

Great question. I used to sit on the roof of my house wondering why life was the way it was. I was about 10 years old when I read National Geographic's story about the ancient Mayans sacrificing young children. I wondered if I had been there. I wondered a lot about everything. I wondered where love fit in.

What I've learned is that if we choose loving, then loving will choose back. I've had plenty of times to choose. I've lost my home to fire. My mother died just a month earlier when my childhood home burned down. I was sued by Social Security for a mistake I reported and have been audited by the IRS! Oh, I forgot to add that my second husband died in an ultra light crash and my ex-husband violated custody and grabbed

144

my daughter out of my hands at school. Sounds pretty nasty. I should add that it all occurred in a short 13 months.

It darn near killed me to deal with all that grief. Grief piled high more quickly than I could process it. In my body's wisdom, I shut down. I went through the motions and mentally grieved. Deep down, though, the losses hadn't been processed; they were stored.

Native Americans have a practice of giving away everything they own. They know that this opens the space for new and even greater gifts to be received. And sometime, they ask for their gifts back! I expect writing this book is my great "give away." What I am receiving back is a reflection of where I've been and who I've become.

Looking back through it all, I know that love walked with me. She stood next to me in the form of friends who gathered together to help. She appeared in the wee hours of the morning when my friend Sally drove to my house and the two of us toasted my husband's passing to the rising sun.

So many acts of kindness lifted me. The tragedies were stepping stones that helped me see that each of us is living love. We are only waiting for life's circumstances to burn away anything that is not. So, hang in there if you are having a tough time. This too shall pass, and love will have her way. Just let her.

Soul Lifts

Here's a toast to love. It will prevail. Light is always stronger than the darkest night.

Here are some clues about finding freedom. Notice when you want something to eat and you're not hungry or you mindlessly smoke, drink or shop. Catch yourself when you wake up and feel lonely or out of sorts. Watch what happens when you get a promotion and after the initial happiness it goes "clunk."

Pay attention to the "clunks" in your life. Spend time getting to know the real you. That's the one beyond the job, the body, the sex or the status. It's even beyond chocolate!

There's a reason that "Know Thyself" was inscribed in the forecourt of the Temple of Apollo at Delphi.

146

Lin Morel

SOUL LIFT #48 The Sound of Freedom

Freedom is to be cherished. So often we put ourselves in cages in order to be part of something. We step on the bandwagon of causes rather than go inside and find our own freedom first.

We are held prisoner by our mind, first and foremost. Our bodies can be crippled, misshapen or drop dead gorgeous as defined by the outside world. The outside world shifts and turns. Emotionally, we can be a prisoner of wanting to be loved. Spiritually, we can be trapped by unexamined dogma.

So what is freedom? To me, freedom is the awareness that true freedom can never be given by the world. The wealthiest people that I know have said that all their money doesn't satisfy the part inside that lacks fulfillment.

Some of the poorest people I know envy those with money, thinking life would be better with cash in the bank. No doubt it would be easier. It just wouldn't be freedom.

Freedom comes when we love ourselves the way we are. No apologies. We are awake enough to see our shortcomings. We are works of art in process. Why not make your life a masterpiece from the inside out? You already are.

147

Soul Lifts

Children see magic everywhere. Magicians rely on slight of hand to create and manipulate effects. Soul magic comes when we allow ourselves to shine the way we are created. All we need to do is get out of our own way. One way to do that is to always ask that everything be for your highest good and the highest good of all concerned.

148

SOUL LIFT #49 Magic Making

If you want some magic in your life start looking. Open your eyes to the magic that is here and now. Take that first step. As Goethe said, "Boldness has genius and power and magic in it."

So be bold, write down what you want, and take your next step toward your goal. Allow providence, your unseen guide, to walk with you toward your destination. Magic is in the moment. Stay present and alert. Miracles and magic go hand in hand.

I challenge you to fill a journal with all the magic moments you encounter. Treasure them, for they are memory makers that will lift you when you feel down and out.

Soul Lifts

Lack of compassion is a sign of a downward spiral into negativity. Beware the dogs of negativity that will nip at your heels. The dogs are judgment, over thinking, expectations and lack of self care.

What one tiny little thing can you do today that will help you become more compassionate toward yourself and others? Remember, compassion begins at home.

SOUL LIFT #50 Compassion Comes to Visit

So, I'm here on Soul Lift #50 and not feeling very compassionate towards myself. My back is sore, I'm tired, judgmental and in need of a nap. Thank goodness for compassion.

Sometimes I'm the least compassionate person I know when it comes to myself. How about you? Do you get down on yourself when things don't go the way you have decided they should go? I do! I call it worshipping the false god of expectation.

Compassion is the antidote to just about everything that ails us. It's the balm that soothes. It comes in the form of a friend who reminds you to be gentle. It comes when you are encouraged not to give up when the going is tough. It even comes in the form of an acquaintance that calls up to remind you that something you've said or done has made a difference.

The biggest difference you and I can make is to practice compassion for ourselves and others. It's caring in action. It's kindness personified. It's giving yourself a break. Again, we're all works of art in progress. So let go, loosen up, and maybe, just maybe, go take a nap. I am.

151

Soul Lifts

"Harmony is pure love, for love is a concerto." Lope de Vega

Grace is loving what you have.

152

SOUL LIFT #51 Harmony and Grace

Harmony soothes the soul at deep levels. It's a pleasing blend of sounds that bring greater peace to all concerned. Music can move people to relax. It can help bring balance and creativity. It can sow discord, disharmony and disrupt your brain's function. There are also certain vibrations that leave peace and open the door for grace to enter.

Think about it for a minute. Have you ever walked into a home and suddenly felt your spirits lift? Notice how we will often say, "This place has good vibes." Do certain songs leave you smiling or lift your spirits when you are low? That's harmony in action.

There is a certain tone that I know of that is said to invoke the divine compassion of the feminine aspect of God. I use it when I am in need of some inner harmony.

It's called "Ani-Hu." Ani (pronounced ahn-eye) invokes compassion, and Hu is an ancient Sanskrit word for God. String the two together and you get an Ahi-Hu. Try it sometime when you are feeling out of sorts. It just might bring you the harmony you've been looking for.

There are lots of sounds that will invoke harmony. Ani-Hu is the one that works best for me. It's not religious in nature. It's a vibration that our body recognizes and responds to. I say it at least three times. If you do it too many times, you may find yourself drifting off to a meditative state. As with anything that softens your focus, it's best not to chant it while you are driving.

153

Soul Lifts

Life is short. What keeps you waiting, always in line, never arriving?

Have you forgotten who you are?

If you knew who you were, who would you be?

154

blessed the grumps along the way. I called a friend spur of the moment and we had tea together. How illogical! I was wasting good time when I could be writing.

By listening to the subtle inner direction, I awoke to the fact that expectations still kept me from knowing my preferences . Acting on the inner direction had been a gift. I'd opened my heart to greater connection, caring and compassion for others and myself.

A walk in the sun, puppies playing with each other, and a cup of tea were just what I needed to fill my heart to overflowing. I was ready to write again.

What about you? Do you take the time to listen and connect with your own inner wisdom?

159

Soul Lifts

"You can't out give God." Edwin Gaines, Unity Minister

SOUL LIFT #54 To Give or Receive

Evangelists have often said it is more blessed to give than receive. Perhaps. I have found if we allow ourselves to gratefully receive from others when they offer us a gift, then we are actually blessing them. We get to be secret givers in our willingness to receive.

Ironically, the window with which we receive determines the window with which we give, and visa versa. Want to have more? Give more.

When someone says, "thank you" for a gift, replying "you're welcome" will complete a cycle of giving and receiving. There can be no giving without receiving and there can be no receiving without giving.

So how about it? Join me in the secret giver's campaign.

161

Soul Lifts

Surprise! This is an appreciation of you, the reader. Thank you for reading my book and passing Soul Lifts along to others. You are now officially part of the Soul Lift Evolution.

162

Life can be pretty simple if you remember that all you need to do is just keep getting up one more time than you fall. Or, as Dorothy Fields wrote in the 1936 movie Swingtime with Fred Astaire and Ginger Rogers, "Pick yourself up, dust yourself off and start all over again!"

It's human to fall, fail and forget who we really are. That goes with having a body. Life is motion. So fall down, fail and forget that you are love, but don't let life's experiences keep you there. When life delivers challenges, you'll build muscles, character and wisdom when you look for the underlying lesson. Go easy on yourself when you go down, forgive yourself for forgetting you are divine, and open up to the mystery of life.

"*We are not human beings having a spiritual experience; we are spiritual beings having a human experience."* Pierre Teilhard de Chardin, Jesuit priest, paleontologist and mystic

173

SOUL LIFT #60 How Come?

If you know so much, how come you have times when you forget and are out of balance?

That's an easy one to answer. If you knew better, you would generally do better. The caveat is that we are human and forget — a lot. The real sign of growth and maturity is not that we are perfect; it's the length of time it takes to remember we are divine having a human experience.

Be gentle, your life isn't done with you yet. There's still more to learn, to do and to become.

If you are breathing, you are still learning.

We are all miracles and works of art in progress. The more you intend to become aware, the more aware you will become. The trick is to be gentle. We already have lions, tigers and bears galore. No need to let the wolves hiding in the shadows nip at your heels and take you down. Instead, turn them into Soul Lifts.

Love yourself because you matter.

POSTSCRIPT

In the end, you will find the beginning...

We find ourselves at 60 Soul Lifts. There are 60 seconds in a minute, and 60 minutes in an hour. I trust this little book has offered you some additional insights to help you exercise your Soul Lifts to navigate the seconds, minutes and hours of your life with more loving.

Life is precious. Love is precious. Love your life on this precious adventure as if it matters. It does.

We are all part of the circle of life. We are an integral part of the fabric that unites our world.

The world would be less without you. So join the circle, join the fun, and let's offer our gifts of loving to the world. For the loving you share is both the beginning and the ending, the alpha and omega.

176

About the Author

Her closest friends describe Dr. Lin as a Renaissance woman. A dedicated student of the martial arts for decades, she's learned that each of us have a connection to a core of power and strength that exists within. A life long learner, traveler and student of indigenous cultures here and abroad, Dr. Lin has created a multi-dimensional process that supports her clients as they awaken to and deepen their relationship their own spiritual connection and inner wisdom.

A former national karate champion and 5th degree black belt, she's also a spiritual director, minister, mother, entrepreneur, and holistic health care practitioner. The thread that crosses every area of her life is her commitment to planting seeds of loving, health and wealth in every heart she meets.

In addition to her work as speaker, trainer and mentor to many, she is actively involved with A Window Between Worlds (AWBW.org). AWBW is a non-profit organization dedicated to using art as a healing tool to empower and transform individuals and communities impacted by violence and trauma.

Dr. Lin is a founding member of the Evolutionary Business Council and was voted International Coach of the Year for her work with individuals and organizations. She has appeared on PBS, NBC, The Discovery Channel, and in the New York Times. Dr Lin is a former member of the National Speaker's Association and the author of several other books and audio programs.

For more information go to www.linmorel.com

Made in the USA
San Bernardino, CA
23 November 2014